My Trade Is Mystery

Seven Meditations from a Life in Writing

CARL PHILLIPS

Yale

UNIVERSITY PRESS

New Haven & London

PUBLISHED WITH ASSISTANCE FROM
THE RONALD AND BETTY MILLER TURNER FUND,
AND FROM THE FOUNDATION ESTABLISHED IN MEMORY OF
AMASA STONE MATHER OF THE CLASS OF 1907, YALE COLLEGE.

Yale University Press books may be purchased in quantity for
educational, business, or promotional use. For information, please e-mail
sales.press@yale.edu (U.S. office) or sales@yaleup.co.uk (U.K. office).

Designed and typeset in Adobe Text by Dustin Kilgore
Printed in the U.S.A.

Library of Congress Control Number: 2022934242

ISBN 978-0-300-25787-8 (hardcover : alk. paper)
ISBN 978-0-300-27414-1 (paperback)

A catalogue record for this book is available from the British Library.

10 9 8 7 6 5 4 3 2 1

MY TRADE IS MYSTERY

For my students

To envy a wilderness, as opposed
to becoming one: he has learned the difference, how
all the more powerful parts to a life—as to art,
as well, when it's worth remembering—resist
translation. Whence comes their power. My
trade is mystery, this song I also call mystery,
he says to himself, half singing.

CONTENTS

MY TRADE IS MYSTERY

Preface

"Each body has its art [that] is its, and nothing else's." This line from Gwendolyn Brooks's sonnet sequence "Gay Chaps at the Bar" speaks of the body's signature, what makes each of us uniquely recognizable as a physical entity. But it could as easily describe the mystery part of this book's title, namely, the mystery component in writing. We can call it voice or style, but ultimately how our writing manifests our sensibility, and why it does so in its particular way, remains a mystery, or—I would say—it should. To acknowledge limits to what we can know about a thing—to acknowledge mystery—is not, to my mind, an admission of defeat by mystery but instead a show of respect for it, and to this extent—I mean this as secularly as possible—it's a form of faith.

So this book doesn't claim to unveil any mysteries about writing. Nor is it a craft book with prompts for generating poems, tips for how to think about poems, et cetera. It began with a suggestion from Sarah Miller, who was overseeing the Yale Series of Younger Poets when I served as series judge. She asked me if I could imagine a book in which I told my students what I thought they might most need to know, not in terms of how to write or to be a writer, but in terms of how to live, *as* a writer.

Unlike my usual way of proceeding when writing a poem, however, I knew I'd have to forgo mystery at least in terms of structure for writing a book of essays. I had to propose a purpose for the book, an imagined market for it, and a feasible structure for it. I knew almost immediately that I wanted seven chapters, and that I wanted them to be easily readable in a single sitting, making the book both portable and inviting. But once I started narrowing down my topics, I realized that they weren't just for students or beginning writers; they applied to writers at every stage of a writing life (which includes career, but doesn't have to; we don't all write for a career, and some with a career—I include myself here—never intended one, and still don't: we just keep needing to write the next poem . . .).

With the exception of one essay ("Politics," which was commissioned by a journal in 2016 and appears here revised down to half its earlier length), all of these essays are original to this book, and were written across a single winter—mostly in Massachusetts; I'd wake up before dawn each morning to continue writing by hand in a notebook. I'm aware that, as often happens when I write a lot in a limited space of time, there are points that recur in more than one essay. Some of these repetitions I revised away. But others I kept, in the hope that, as the context in which these points reappear changes, the effect will be not redundancy but something more akin to those notes and chords that, in music, make up the motif that returns at various points across a composition to provide structure, the patterning without which music would be mere noise.

What follows are chapters, or essays, or what I've called meditations. They're meant not as proof of a thing but as invitations to consider a topic, provocations for further—and ever changing—consideration. They're also personal, insofar as I can only speak from the context of all the experiences I've accumulated. But when I say personal, I mean that these pieces—like my poems—are invested less in a presentation of self than in an interrogation of that self and its relationship to the world I inhabit; I'm also always interrogating the world itself, versus what I've called the world, versus how I think of it.

A word about the title. It comes from a poem of mine, an excerpt from which includes the title and serves as my epigraph for this book. I don't actually think of the writing of poetry (or any literary writing) as a trade—it's just what I do. It does have some rules—flexible though they may be—there *is* such a thing as technique, as with all trades. But why we decide to make things from words, why words as opposed to another medium—that's a mystery, as is all the rest that isn't teachable, but which distinguishes some poems from others, makes them memorable, muscular, living, felt, and leaves us as readers feeling we've been for a moment differently alive, and forever changed. Poems, for me, are deeply private, as is the making of them. I've no idea how I do this thing, ultimately. Nor do I want to know. To be given a map or compass would prevent my getting lost—what, for me, the making of poems requires from the start; the act of writing is a way of finding a way forward into the next clearing, as temporary stay against the inevitable next stretch of wilderness, where with luck the next poem lies hidden.

But a writing life is a separate thing from the writing. If writing is an ongoing quest—and I believe it is—then this book is meant as a guide for navigating the various distractions that hinder the writing (and sometimes the life), things that we're all susceptible to, like self-doubt, a feeling of having nothing left to say, a fear that we're somehow not doing this thing "correctly." There's no single correct way. What I offer here are some thoughts not on how to vanquish various demons and distractions, but on how to negotiate a healthy relationship with them, given that—even thirty years or so later—they don't go away: they tend rather to wax and wane without any pattern that I've been able to find.

I set out to write the book that I'd have wanted to read when I first started writing, when I knew no living writers, had no community as guide or sounding board or support. But in the course of writing it, I found that this is a book I also need now, maybe more than ever. I don't want instruction—didn't want it when I started, either; I want companionship, a partner in speculation, a reminder in my alonest moments that I'm not alone entirely. I want intimacy. I adore economy. I require precision. I know the light and the shadows are definitionless without each other. Clarity and insight don't have to compromise mystery. Here, the road shifts a bit, feels steeper. Take my hand, in the dark.

AMBITION

"That's all that happens, I think, we stop moving forever." So I said once, in a poem, to describe death. By that logic, life equals motion, we are as human beings by definition restless, dissatisfaction becomes a form of survival, to be dissatisfied with an empty stomach triggers an instinct to fill that emptiness with what in turn enables us to live a while longer. We resist dissatisfaction as we resist shapelessness; the impulse to know a thing—another form of survival—is an impulse toward recognizability, we give shape to shapelessness, and we call it meaning. And it feels like arrival. We forget for a moment that meaning itself is unfixed, ever changing. And the forgetting—isn't this, too, survival?

I've often been asked if art is necessary. And for years my standard answer was that art isn't required for survival, but it gives an added dimension to life, without which life would be—what, less appealing? Boring? But, for reasons I'll never know, making art is how some of us make sense of the world for ourselves; it's absolutely, then, a means of survival, which makes it necessary. A poem may not be how I stave off physical hunger, but if it's how I temporarily arrive at something like clarity and stability—emotionally, psychologically, intellectually—then yes, I need it. Art is one of many ways to get there but for the artist it's a chief way, and sometimes the only way. To this extent, there's truth to the idea of art-making as vocation, a natural calling. It's easy, though, for elitism to creep into this way of thinking: the idea that some are called, and others are not, or, as Alfred Corn puts it, speaking of making a career in poetry, in his highly regarded manual on prosody:

> All you have to do then is go on to produce complete
> and unified poems in which every line contains its depth
> charge of technical/intuitive insight. A tall order? Yes, as
> tall as Mount Parnassus, to whose slopes many are called
> but few are chosen.
>
> —*The Poem's Heartbeat*

To be clear from the start, I believe anyone who chooses to make art has the right to do so, and has the right to define art for themselves. Some make that choice, others don't. Neither choice is wrong or better. (For further clarification, I'm speaking here of what traditionally gets called the arts—literature, music, dance, painting, sculpting, etc. For there's an art to pretty much everything, from digging a trench to changing a diaper to tree climbing.)

There's a distinction, though, between the hobbyist and the artist for whom there is no other way. I wrote poems off and on, in high school. I continued writing here and there in college and even served on the college poetry magazine staff. Then I stopped for almost ten years, during which it never really occurred to me to write; I certainly didn't miss it. But when I did finally start writing again, the writing—though I didn't know this at the time—was the medium by which I wrestled my way toward a clarity about something I couldn't understand in any other way, my own queerness, which seems obvious to me now, but which I'd somehow suppressed, not been ready for, had suspected and turned away from as from a childhood monster the child hopes to make disappear by closing his eyes. To write poems felt like finding the native language of my interior self, and discovering that I'd always known this language—I had only to speak it: so *this* is my name; and this here, who I am.

Because the artist makes art out of necessity—almost as if by instinct—ambition may seem at first out of place, but this is mostly because people too easily confuse ambition with competition. The first sense in which I want to speak of ambition,

though, has nothing to do with other people and their per-
ceptions. Rather, the committed artist is driven by the human
restlessness mentioned earlier, is constantly evolving, finding
patterns, settling into some of them, abandoning others, in
search of yet another way to approach (as opposed to resolving) the conundrums that have been the catalyst for making
art all along. As Stanley Kunitz says in his poem "Touch Me":
"What makes the engine go? / Desire, desire, desire." And
this desire is a manifestation of ambition, an ambition for the
work—the art—to capture what can't be captured otherwise,
and even then can't be captured entirely; which is to say,
defeat is built into the mechanism. For example, let's say I'm in
love. So I write a love poem that depicts love as easy, blissful,
because that's my experience of love. Then the relationship
doesn't work out and I realize my love poem has failed to get
at the disappointment that love can bring. So I write a new
poem, and this time I'm convinced I've nailed it—"it" being
the whole subject of love. Twenty years and three relation-
ships later, I understand that not only do love and its joys and
disappointments vary according to the relationship, but that
I myself have been changing the entire time as well, so what
love looked like to me at forty is nothing like how it looks at
sixty.

All art springs from a human impulse, if not to resolve what's
not resolvable, then to contain, if only temporarily, what

resists containment—in this case, love, which can be seen as a many-faceted piece of quartz, let's say, held up and turned, turning in a shifting light, so that the light hits some facets, misses others, each time differently. The poem seeks to capture the light as it hits a given facet—but that doesn't describe the whole, just a fleeting piece of it. Ambition understands that, and refuses it. Each time I write a poem, I feel as if I've laid something to rest, arrived at the stability of having understood a thing. But the satisfaction is temporary, since what I sought to hold in place is as restless as I am. So, whatever the poem has succeeded in capturing, it's also failed to capture every aspect. There lies the defeat I spoke of. But ambition, instead of seeing defeat as failure and succumbing to frustration, treats defeat as a necessary step toward the next poem that will surely, *this* time, get it right. Except there *is* no right. There's just the ever-questing-forward, believing as firmly in art's powers of resolution as the knights of old believed, apparently, in the Holy Grail. In this way, ambition is a form of faith, a belief in any given subject's knowability, a belief in art's ability to know.

Since the artist is ever evolving, and as art's subject matter is simultaneously ever evolving and ever elusive, it makes sense that the medium itself must keep evolving. How we express ourselves and understand ourselves and the world around us is mostly via our individual sensibilities, which shift and deepen

11

with experience over time. Why shouldn't art—the artist's medium for understanding and expression—change accordingly? Some of this happens naturally, just as our understanding of love (to return to my earlier example) changes without our ever having to do more than continue living and trying to love. There's also, though, a more intentional, if often unconscious, ambition for the work, one that can be understood at the level of craft. I used to write poems in short-lined, three-line stanzas; later, I wrote single-stanza poems made of long lines that made some readers think the poems were in fact prose poems, meaning they had abandoned line breaks. This shift became apparent only in hindsight—I made no conscious choice, that I remember, to change the way my poems looked. At some point the form I'd settled on became too easy, inadequate, but mostly unsurprising. We think of ambition as a hunger for more; I think of it mainly as a hunger for difference, a hunger that's ultimately also strategic: if the quest is to get closer to what forever just eludes our grasp, and if the poem—in my own case—is my attempt to capture an ever shifting subject or idea ("to catch the world / at pure idea," Jorie Graham has said), then my tools for capturing will need to adjust according to the latest nature of my subject. The right tool for the right job, is another way of putting it. The way epic accommodates story better than a sonnet does. The way a sail is preferable to a net, for catching the wind.

Revision is another word for this particular kind of ambition for the work. This includes not just the usual idea of revision— changing a word here, adding a semicolon there—but revision as a new way of seeing, what the word means originally, to see again but also differently. What does using long lines to grapple with an idea look like, versus using short lines? What different thing will be revealed, what same thing will be differently revealed?

I never intended a career as a poet. Pretty much since graduating from college I've dedicated myself to teaching, and it's been my career for over forty years now. When, as a high school Latin teacher, I began writing the poems that would come together as my first book, I had no real knowledge of contemporary poetry, let alone journals for poetry, contests, reviews, the "business" of poetry. Even though I couldn't know this then, it was the only time I'd ever write poems with absolutely no sense of audience, and therefore no expectations of one. I wrote poems from necessity—yes, as a form of therapy, as I got closer to understanding the sexuality I was too afraid of, in myself, to confront otherwise. Which is to say, the last thing on my mind was publication. Then came a summer when I discovered the first books of Lucie Brock-Broido, Marie Howe, and Brigit Pegeen Kelly, my first books of contemporary poetry. I loved them. And I saw that each book included a page of acknowledgments of where the poems had first appeared. And that was the first time I can remember thinking that I might try sending my own poems to a journal—to these journals, which must be good, because they'd published work I admired. There began yet another form of ambition, as powerful as it is dangerous, or can be: the desire to show one's work to the world, which (despite my wanting to think of it as an act of generosity, another form of teaching) is finally a desire for approval, the desire to be valued and, by extension, though the two are not the same, to be loved.

The dangers of this form of ambition are many. Its first strategy is to seduce by distorting logic: "If I'm published in a magazine, I'll be a real writer." It becomes quickly addictive: "If my poems could be published as a book, I'll truly have made it" leads easily to "If my book wins a prize, I'll be the 'best' writer, having triumphed over all the other contenders." I believe very few artists avoid falling into some version of this thinking from time to time. As artists, we have something to say, and because we are saying it, it feels—it *is*—personal, which makes us vulnerable, which in turn makes us long for the protection that, at first, public approbation feels like, protection ultimately from our own fears and doubts as to our "worthiness," our "right" to call ourselves an artist, maybe even a good one.

But approval is *not* protection, when it comes to art.

I used to equate winning a prize for writing with winning Wimbledon, but that's not right. Putting aside the possibility of bad calls by referees, putting aside luck—good and bad— to win Wimbledon is to have played the best game of tennis, albeit only on that particular day; today's champion could as easily be defeated tomorrow by the one who lost today. But winning a prize for art, far from meaning you were the best today, really just means that a randomly assembled group of humans and therefore subjective and each-with-their-own-biases judges came to an agreement—itself often uneasy—that your art was deserving of a prize. That doesn't make it the best or, to be absolutely honest, even good.

Prizes are part of the politics that attend art the way flies attend horses. They ultimately distract from what, as far as I can tell, art is mostly about: the urgency of and devotion to and sheer pleasure in the act of making some form of expression for what it means to be alive in a human body at this moment in time.

I often remind my students of what making a career in writing maybe most requires, besides luck, some talent, and stamina: a constant calibrating and recalibrating of arrogance and humility. You need the arrogance to believe not only that you have something to say but that the world must hear it; and you need the humility to recognize both that not everyone wants to listen and that no one is in fact obligated to do so. This too seems part of the work of ambition.

A steady drive, without expectation. An acceptance that to be an artist is to commit to a lifelong apprenticeship to mastery over what cannot truly be mastered, since the definition of art—as with the evaluation of excellence—is ever shifting and always subjective. Accepting the fact of this—indeed, even embracing it—will return you to that most important form of ambition that I mentioned earlier, the ambition for the work. When it comes to the art itself, a prize is already irrelevant because it's (usually) for work that's finished; the committed artist will already have continued that fumbling forward into the unknown that is finally required for the work to keep deepening, to continue surprising. This ambition will keep your mind on the work, what matters most; as much as possible, let the work be everything; for the work will save you.

STAMINA

As with most things when decided upon at first—a beloved, a political cause, or, in my own case, the writing of poems—it's easy to think all we have to do is start doing: show love, be politically alert, write poems. Maybe one of the chief values of enthusiasm is its ability to simultaneously energize us toward commitment and render us usefully—for the time—oblivious to the sheer stamina that sustained commitment, what we call a career, requires. Shortly after my first book was published, a teacher of mine told me that having a career in poetry was like riding a runaway open streetcar, that the secret was to hold on tightly and stay aboard, rather than becoming one of the many who get thrown off, into the street. "Keep watching, you'll see what I mean," he said. I remember being amused and more than a little horrified by this image, but I've come to understand the general idea, and I don't disagree, not entirely. Thinking back to all of the writers who started publishing around the same time as I did, there are so many whose voices I had thought would be the dominant ones for decades to come—yet they fell silent or, if not silent, never matched or in any way came close to the achievement for which they were earlier acclaimed. There are just as many others whose voices seemed negligible to me, whose work I'd still call unsurprising, yet it continues, like the writers themselves, to thrive and be published widely. And there is a third group, of modest accomplishment at the start, who have managed to differently surprise me by becoming better. I now see how much more powerful stamina can be than talent; or, to say it another way, how powerless talent is, on its own, without stamina—rather like what is said about the body once the soul has left it, though I don't believe in the soul. I do believe in stamina.

Stamina, at least at first, presumes ambition. If ambition is what makes us want to write at all, for example, stamina is what sustains that drive or desire over time in the face of the many things that can sometimes thwart ambition and sometimes utterly destroy it. Stamina has its limitations, of course; it's not much use against the certainty of death and, before that, the unpredictability of physical and mental health. But if ambition is, as I've suggested earlier, a form of faith, then stamina is what comes into play when that faith—as it will, inevitably—gets shaken. Stamina is the persistence by which we move past doubt and return to the task of making. But when we're in doubt, it's not always as simple to just "move on" or "get over it." Which is to say, stamina is not just persistence; stamina, in the way that I'm thinking of it, always includes perspective, the means by which we can contextualize doubt and, in giving it context, displace it somewhat, thereby clearing room again for shaken faith. Maybe the best way to think of stamina is as a fusion of perspective and will.

Too much or too little attention paid from outside—by readers, critics—is a leading cause of doubt when it comes to ambition. Granted, much of this will depend on the individual. To receive a lot of favorable attention to a first book, say, can spur some writers to work confidently toward the second book, but for others it can create the pressure of expectation: can I do this again, can I keep doing it, at just as praiseworthy a level, over many years? Conversely, sometimes the attention received is disproportionately negative—and again, different artists respond differently: some, believing the negative attention, fall silent, humiliated at having been, as they'd feared, "found out," while others, convinced that the reviewers and readers are all of them wrong, set out to prove it by writing the next book as evidence.

Stamina's essential, though, to each of these scenarios, if we're to move past these mostly psychological and emotional obstacles. "I can't go on. I'll go on," goes the line from Beckett's

The Unnamable. Stamina's what happens between those two sentences. It reminds me, whether the attention to a given book has been good or bad, (1) that the book itself existed and meant something to me long before anyone else confirmed its existence or worth, and (2) that each book is itself, that the point is for me to find my way, undistracted, toward the book that I have to write, for me—only I need to find it praiseworthy; likewise, if I've failed to write the book I must write, only I can know that, it's for me to say. Of course, when the attention has been negative, it's harder to think this way, and it may take a bit longer for stamina to kick in, as it were; negative attention—or no attention—to what we've worked hard to make from and of our deepest selves hurts, quite a lot, initially. But the perspective that stamina includes helps me to remember points one and two, above. It also makes me mindful of one of the artist's tasks, mentioned earlier: the necessary and ongoing calibration of arrogance and humility that helps the artist distinguish ambition for the work from the endlessly hungry, other ambition for public approval. Take praise when and if you can get it, but don't forget that it was never the point—or, if it was, then you've confused devotion with celebrity, which is a sometime by-product of the devotion that the committed making of art equals, but celebrity has nothing to do, in the end, with the making of art, let alone its value.

In the dream, I lived alone with an old dog in an abandoned

filling station, as they used to call them. The dog, whose hind legs were becoming daily more useless to him, suddenly leapt with ease onto a countertop and looked me in the eye. "Wait—how'd you do that?" I asked him. "I wanted to see the world from where you are, from your perspective," the dog said. Sometimes I think the dream is about reading, other times about the readers we write toward, a small hand against disappearance, not the gull but its reflection moving steadily across the water's—for now—windless surface . . .

There's also a kind of stamina that doesn't, initially, involve perspective at all, a stamina fueled by urgency, which is to stamina as adrenaline is to the body, enabling us, for a moment, to perform at levels we didn't know we were capable of, or that we take at the time for granted.

For me, urgency's always involved, at some level, when I'm writing, or at least a feeling of necessity, something needs to be expressed. But the kind of urgency I mean here is more extreme, where the urgency feels impossible to ignore, it crowds everything else from view, until there's only urgency and the imperative to write a way through it. That's where stamina comes in. I've only known this form of urgency twice so far in my writing life. The first was when I was writing the poems for what would become my first book. As I've mentioned, the urgency had to do with a conundrum of sexuality;

I'd come to believe that my life quite literally depended on my resolving that conundrum. Resolving it was as "simple" as acknowledging my being a gay man, but that was hardly simple, between how I'd been raised and the times as they were, between my being married at the time to a woman whom I truly loved and my having found myself sexually involved with—and yes, in love with, though love was nowhere in fact part of it—a man I'd turned to for help in my confusion.

Without planning to, I began writing several poems each weekend (the only time my job allowed for writing), many of which got written in a single sitting without revision. I can be skeptical of this way of proceeding when I see it in my students, yet I've been there myself, when all that matters is to write until I can't. It violates Wordsworth's "sacred"—though somewhat contradictory—idea that poetry is "the spontaneous overflow of powerful feelings" and at the same time "takes its origin from emotion recollected in tranquility." Or maybe I had, in fact, had enough years to reflect, even if subconsciously, on my feelings by having lived with them long enough inside, and what felt like spontaneous outbursts had actually been long in the making, getting steadily revised along the way—who can say?

For the poems that I wrote weren't bald confessions. Though I'd not yet studied poetry writing, some part of me seems to have understood instinctively what Ellen Bryant Voigt told me many years later: that poetry is not the transcription but the transformation of experience. I wrote the poems of my first book in my late twenties. I'd had enough time—even if only barely enough—both to have accumulated experiences and to have begun thinking past the fact of those experiences to what's more difficult, what together they might mean.

The urgency behind that first book felt like writing to save my life. The only other time I've experienced that urgency was in the immediate wake of my coming out, which coincided with (1) meeting a man who became my partner for almost eighteen years and (2) my getting divorced and consequently trying to reconcile doubts about faith and commitment with my determination to forge a lasting relationship with a man, the kind of relationship I'd grown up thinking was immoral and therefore impossible. I was writing now not to save my life, but to find a sturdy enough shape for it. By then my first book had been published and I'd been admitted to a writing program that provided a year to do pretty much nothing but write; and I'd say I wrote four to five poems a week for that entire year.

Stamina—sheer will—produced the poems of these two periods, but in both of them a particular urgency, a crisis of identity, lay behind the stamina, and was the catalyst for a pro-

STAMINA

ductivity I've not known since. If we're lucky, though, crisis doesn't govern every moment of our lives. And while a large part of the urgency of that period of my life had to do with sexual identity, I can't overlook the urgency, as well, of youth itself. I wasn't yet thirty-two during the periods I've mentioned. Our twenties and thirties, for most of us, are the time when we're just coming into a sense of who we are as adults; the different freedom of adulthood (for childhood, too, has its freedoms, as does adolescence, despite how it feels) combined with the recent maturing of our thinking—about ourselves, about the world around us—means we have a lot to say, all of it still new, and we have the energy to say it. I remember feeling, at the time, that I couldn't write fast enough to get all of my thoughts down.

I once heard Geoffrey Hill speak about the role of tension in poetry—specifically, he said the poet must have something to push up against. I agree. Earlier, for me, I'd say I was pushing against societal conventions about sexual identity, figuring out how to make a space for someone like me who didn't "fit" convention. But having understood my sexuality, I no longer needed to write about trying to understand it. That would be redundant. Meanwhile, youth fades, as do the energies that came with it. So the challenge is how to maintain stamina, past youth, and without having to be routinely visited by crisis. It helps to remember that urgency doesn't have to mean crisis.

24

Simply to interrogate an idea or event is a form of that pushing against that Hill argues for. And to the degree that you have a stake in that interrogation, there *is* an urgency to it, for *you*. For example, say you want to write a sequence of poems on the life of Billie Holiday. Presumably you've read enough to know the basic biography. So, in deciding to take on this subject, you should either have something new to say about it—to add, revise, contradict—or have come upon a new way to say what's already been said. This means you're pushing against either received information or conventions of form, respectively. This isn't crisis, but it is resistance, and that, combined with your personal investment in that resistance, is a form of urgency, which is in turn a catalyst for you to get the poems written—a catalyst, that is, for stamina.

(Utterance itself is a form of resistance against silence.)

Meanwhile, we get older. And if we've continued writing and arrived at something like a career, the act of writing has become habit, a way of life. We may still have much to say, but we've also said many things already. How to avoid repeating ourselves, how to keep seeing things anew, how to separate habit from habit's predictability—and how find the stamina to do so? I think this is where self-awareness—about ourselves, yes, but also about the work—is key. I've written plenty of poems that interested me but later, sometimes minutes after finishing them, sometimes months, I'll realize I've merely echoed what I've written somewhere else before. Or I've used an image I've used often—fair enough—but I haven't used it any differently than I have before. For me those poems aren't worth holding on to. That doesn't mean they weren't worth writing, since everything we write is a necessary step to the poems we need to write, but I don't find that I need to publish them. This may be the most important requirement for a career, the ability to look at one's own work with enough detachment to be a useful monitor and critic of the work, across decades.

At the same time, it's encouraging to know that with age, in tandem with experience, our sensibilities deepen, which means that we don't have to work at constantly changing how we see the world—that changes anyway, as does the world itself. A certain amount of the work of avoiding redundancy is just part of being alive. I've written quite a bit about the body, about sex in particular, but each time I've done so from within a different body, a body that isn't as young as it once was, but is much more practiced, as well, much more understood as my own. Necessarily, though sometimes subtly, the poems have changed over time.

For me, both as reader and writer, a piece of writing (but again, the same for all art) is only as interesting as its capacity for surprise. And it's the possibility of surprise—the firm belief in that possibility—that keeps me reading and writing. Which is to say, it encourages stamina, a drive to keep moving forward, perhaps at a different pace as I get older, perhaps no longer in the grip of crisis, but I'm moving forward. The journey has its own pleasures, as does having arrived—which has less, I think, to do with my being an artist than with my commitment to living deeply, mindfully, and without complacency. Can't that too, though, be a definition, at least part of it, for the artistic life?

To write poems that make a meaningful difference, that do the transformative work of showing readers (and myself as the writer) the world in a new way—this is difficult, yes. But the chance for surprise makes the work inviting. Difficulty, surprise—maybe that's all a career comes down to. Difficulty meets surprise, and—without having thought to choose to— they mate for life.

SILENCE

I woke early—looked up, then out, out into the un-silence that I call silence, what maybe doesn't exist. Here, in a stand of woods by the sea, where for company there's just the small squadron of wild turkeys negotiating the backyard's sloped geometry of pines and oak trees, it's easy enough not only to confuse isolation with silence, but to rise and strut from the house naked, unconfused, and say aloud to no one, "Why not, who's to stop me, if I call it silence?" In this way, silence is a lot like writing, I think: relative, and private, powerful in its intimacy, which has its own power to be deployed or with-held, depending—maybe equally?—on the writer and on what those encountering what I've written might be willing to bring to it, whom I'll never know.

———

Silence—as in the absence of sound—is an invention of those who can hear, says Ilya Kaminsky: "The deaf don't believe in silence." How do we understand sound, except in relationship to its absence? We know sound by what is not sound, and vice versa. But how can a thing be absent—to ourselves, anyway—if we've never known it? Which is to say, I agree with Ilya, and what I mean more and more by silence is the relative absence of distraction, or of the usual distractions. I'm writing here in the absence of city distractions that include people, traffic, and the low-grade, habitual alertness to potential danger that seems to come with urban living. But from my window, I can see wildlife, how the trees are a map of the wind's motion, what's left of a winter storm heading out to sea. These too are distractions, but not the usual ones, so that being here feels like escape, when it's just a difference.

So, silence not as an absence of sound, and not necessarily as an absence of distraction. Maybe any space, psychologically, that allows our attention to a thing to manifest itself as art. For me, that has required a relative absence of any human-related sound, but I also understand how for others it can mean writing in a noisy coffee shop filled with people, as if the noise were catalyst for a private interiority within which to pay attention to what no one else in the room can know unless we choose to *make* it known.

I think that's all art is, a record of interior attention paid. Is this what Horace meant, about poetry being like a picture? I think so. The pictures are various—a picture of what no one else can understand, or more often a picture of what others do in fact understand but can never understand quite as we do, through the personal lens of our own individual experiences of the world, which is to say art presents the world both all over again and—even if only slightly, sometimes—anew, made strange.

How—oblivious to my watching it from my window—the red-tailed hawk tore open some sort of rodent, a vole, maybe, and ate it alive.
How in ancient Greek the word for "to see" is the word for "to know."
How I've mistakenly, romantically, thought I'll miss this world when I'm dead.
The dead don't miss the world. They can't.
The dead don't miss us.

———

X as signature, proof I was here. I assume the ancient custom still holds, a way for those who can't read or write to sign a document. When I was much younger, a core part of elementary education was learning to write in cursive according to the Palmer method. The cursive alphabet ran across a banner above the chalkboard, and each day included having to copy the letters, in upper and lower case, on specially ruled paper. Only now do I understand this as a way of imposing uniformity—if not on expression itself, then on the medium for it. And yet, when I think back to my days as a high school teacher, what I most remember is the distinctiveness—for better and worse, in terms of legibility—of my students' handwriting. The same is true of my peers. Proof, maybe, of individuality's stubborn insistence upon itself? Why can't that also be what's meant by style or voice or sensibility when it comes to poems, for example? The poem as signature, as personal record or confirmation—of the poem's immediate subject, yes, but also of the poet's having existed: this small manifestation of a moment of private attention to a thing as proof. In this way, to make art is also, like handwriting, a form of insistence. A form, too, of resistance. To write is to resist invisibility. By having spoken, I've resisted silence before again returning to it.

———

I've long been fascinated with the role of the first poem in a poet's first book. It's a bit like the literary equivalent of attending one's first debutante ball (or at least as I can imagine such things, never having attended one)—a similar deliberateness and purposefulness. It's how we announce ourselves to potential strangers for the very first time. "X" is my first book's opening poem, which ends with this sentence: "X is all I keep meaning / to cross out." The signature of X as confirmation and assertion. The implied unease with or regret about that assertion, hence the intention—routinely untended to—of crossing everything out. What it means to keep meaning to, and not doing it. The will to continue, to survive, in spite of. In spite of what?

———

A silence opens, says Amy Clampitt. The title of her final book of poems. I've always taken the title to mean that a silence, having occurred, then expands into something larger, a more encompassing form of itself. But of course, to open can also be transitive, can have agency, so that by silence opening can be meant that a silence opens something else, left unspecified by Clampitt. Why haven't I thought of that, until now?

———

Then there is the silence that others call writer's block, when whatever inside us that allows us to make art falls silent, or a silence settles in around it, preventing our usual access to power, the muse, creativity, imagination. I've never been comfortable with the term "writer's block," with its suggestion of obstacles and combativeness. As with teaching (which in academia too often seems to get confused with correction and oneupsmanship), I prefer to see writing as an invitation. The absence of an invitation doesn't have to mean we've been shunned; instead, maybe there aren't any events on the immediate horizon; or some part of us (the writing part?) realizes we're not ready for these events. In which case, aren't there plenty of other things to do, or that need doing? So maybe the first response to this particular version of silence is to revise how we think of it—less as an obstacle, and more as a shift of attention and energy; right now, actual writing doesn't require us, but—for example—the kitchen floor could use some attention, the dog wouldn't mind a longer walk than usual, when did I last make pizza dough from scratch? This brings me to my second point: the potential value of distraction. Sometimes the problem is that we're trying too hard, too self-consciously, to write, we're too focused on a goal we've set for ourselves, when—contrary to what capitalism would have us believe— art isn't a goal to be checked from a list of goals, any more than art's value can ever be objectively codified like a kind of math; for me, at least, art is the result of my having allowed myself to stray from any marked path and to become lost. The poem is the evidence—like tracks, or footprints—of my quest into and across strange territory, the shape I've left almost as if unintentionally behind me.

Distractions can be useful, then, for pulling us away from self-consciousness about making, and for increasing instead the chances for the seeming accident that, even now, after so many years, each new poem feels like. To this day, my best lines or parts of lines almost always come to me unbidden while I'm walking my dog or doing some of the so-called mindless work of cooking, peeling carrots, mincing the garlic. When this happens, I write the idea down immediately for later. This means that later, when I actually have time to sit down and try writing, I'll be spared the intimidation of the blank page; I'll have something to at least start with, and if those aren't the right lines, they may well be the spark for them.

Finally, it's worth rethinking what we mean by writing—or any act of art making. Is it only writing when we have a pen in hand, or a nearby keyboard? I think writing includes much more than that: patience, attention, openness to the world past screen or page—to what's findable there. These are, if not the act of writing itself, among the conditions, at least, that writing requires.

As long as I am living in language, as I like to put it, I count it as writing. This is why reading, for example, is so important—is maybe the most important part of writing. If I'm reading, I'm also at some level taking in language's capacities and variations for the expression of human experience. Reading

Woolf's sentences won't make me write like Woolf—I can't do that, and I don't want to—but it allows me to engage with sentence strategies that aren't mine and to add those strategies to the many I've acquired all my life by reading. Again, figuring out and imitating a writing strategy from another writer doesn't mean you'll write like that author. Individual sensibility is what makes Woolf who she is. When we adopt another's strategy, we still end up deploying it via our own unique sensibility, which means the sentence we make as a result will remain our own.

Living in language isn't limited to "literary" reading, by the way. For me, it all counts: humming to and trying to catch a song's lyrics; double checking a recipe's detailed instructions before proceeding; scrolling Twitter and getting caught up in a thread on how people used to carve images onto reindeer antlers in the Paleolithic age. Living in language includes what's casually overheard. I remember my first visit to the Soulard Farmers Market, what's billed as the oldest open-air market not just in Saint Louis but in the United States. "Sweeter than mother's love!" one vendor kept shouting, hawking what turned out to be a pile of watermelons, honeydew, and two I couldn't quite identify, but I bought them, sure, and yes, when split open, weren't they sweet, weren't the colors too, inside . . .

Meanwhile, given that everything we write comes to us via the many lenses of the experiences we've accumulated across a life—we speak of trees, for example, according to what we know of trees by actual experience and through what we've experienced of trees in books, movies, nursery rhymes, and more—then everything we do is at some level research for the next poem. The key, I think, to this kind of research is again to keep it from being too self-conscious. To go to the beach, for example, and feel a need to take mental notes the entire time for the next poem is not what I mean. I mean simply going to the beach, maybe swimming, maybe not, listening to the gulls, falling asleep to the sound of waves, noticing how the fog at sunset makes the sunset less and more the point at the same time . . . In my own experience, this rarely translates into a poem "about" going to the beach. But what I felt there, something my brain stored that I don't remember at the time seeing, smelling, or having heard—these are the things that end up appearing in a poem, often years later, and often I myself can't trace my own idea back to its catalyst. I'll admit, it is hard to explain this to university deans who ask me to quantify and itemize the research I've "conducted" while on sabbatical— equally difficult, explaining to a partner who's been watching me apparently just stare out a window for ten minutes that this is part of the business of making. Difficulty explaining a fact, though, doesn't change the fact.

I wrote a poem, once, where two people are riding on horse-
back through a vaguely surreal landscape punctuated by the
occasional flying, beheaded creature. Eventually, for variety's
sake, the two riders dismount and walk for a while, and the
poem ends this way: "We mapped our way north by the stars,
old school, until there / were no stars, just the weather of
childhood, where it's snowing forever." That ending came to
me out of nowhere, and quickly, and seemed absolutely the
only ending. What is the weather of childhood? Is it psychological? Is the snow? Maybe months later, while reading the
poem before an audience, I remembered the dream I used to
have fairly routinely when I was a boy: I've flown with my
mother to the North Pole, and we've gotten separated. I set
out to find her, but there's nothing but snow everywhere, in
drifts towering over me, whenever I call for her the snow that
keeps falling absorbs the sound, I can barely see anymore—I
begin to panic . . .

———

I once asked Ellen Bryant Voigt, a poet for whom there are
typically many years between books of poems, how she han-
dled the silence, what I still thought of at the time as writer's block. "That's not how I think of it," she responded, and
went on to explain to me how a snake, in order to attack, must
first recoil to establish a position from which to attack. As I

understand the analogy, the attack is the act of writing, and the period of recoil, of retraction, is many things: reflection, thinking, revision of thought, remembering. "You're not blocked," Ellen told me. "You're waiting. You're paying attention." Which is also research. Also, a version of silence, the only sound the sound of a snake breathing, which must be, as sounds go, a soft, a small one.

In her poem "[evening and my dead once husband]," Lucille Clifton encounters her dead husband, and presumably believing that old adage about the dead acquiring a wisdom beyond that of the living, she asks him to explain her own anxiety, the fact of illness, the "terrible loneliness / and wars against our people." And instead of answering aloud, he spells out with his fingers "it does not help to know." Indeed. Exactly. Is it maybe better not just to respect but to committedly embrace knowing's limits? Past which, like the sea where the land gives out, yes: a silence opens.

POLITICS

When my first book of poems, *In the Blood,* came out in 1992,
I learned what it could mean to be seen as a political poet for
no other reason than because of who or what one is. Rachel
Hadas, who selected the book for publication, wrote a won-
derful and uncannily accurate introduction, from which the
publisher excerpted the following for the back cover:

> Internal evidence would seem to indicate that [this] is a
> poet of color who is erotically drawn to other men. The
> reductiveness of such terms is one lesson of *In the Blood,*
> with its . . . constant dissolving of one world into another.

I say uncannily accurate, because I had yet to acknowledge to
myself, let alone others, my being gay; about the color part,
I'd been pretty aware, of course, all my life. Sexuality would
end up being the primary lens through which my early work
got read; and given how relatively new it still was to speak

POLITICS

of queerness openly, and given the relative newness of—and
unknown-ness about—HIV and AIDS, the poems were seen
as particularly relevant: political, let's say.

As for color—Blackness—there are only two poems in the
book that speak to this subject specifically (or as others have
put it, there are only two "Black poems" in the book). The
first, "Passing," is a kind of resistance to being told that Black
experience has to come down to a single experience:

> The Famous Black Poet is
> speaking of the dark river in the mind
> that runs thick with the heroes of color,
> Jackie R., Bessie, Billie, Mr. Paige, anyone
> who knew how to sing or when to run.
> I think of my grandmother, said
> to have dropped dead from the evil eye,
> of my lesbian aunt who saw cancer and
> a generally difficult future headed her way
> in the still water
> of her brother's commode.
> I think of voodoo in the bottoms of soup-cans,
> and I want to tell the poet that the blues
> is *not* my name, that Alabama
> is something I cannot use
> in my business.

42

In the other poem, "Blue," the child of a biracial couple—one Black, one White (a k a, me)—speaks of a space between the two, a space of individuality, where it becomes possible to be left alone to pull "my own stoop- / shouldered kind of blues across paper."

But at no point did I think of myself as having an agenda that could be called political. Rather, my agenda, to the extent that it can even be called that, has always been to speak as honestly as possible to my own experience of negotiating and navigating a life as myself, as *a* self—multifarious, restless, necessarily ever changing as the many factors of merely being also change—in a world of selves. Which is to say, I was simply being myself in those first poems—what other choice is there? But I became a poet who, according to reviews, spoke unabashedly—daringly, even—of what many wouldn't, in terms of sex; as for race, I'd unknowingly thrown a gauntlet down to a long tradition of assumptions as to what Blackness meant and especially as to how a poet of color should speak, and about what.

———

There are countless aspects to a self; race and sexual orientation are only two of them, it seems to me, neither the least nor the most important. It's more accurate to say there's a constant

43

shifting of hierarchy, depending on any given moment in experience. Am I a gay Black man when roasting a chicken at home for friends? Sure. But that's not what I'm most conscious of, at the time. Am I necessarily, then, stripped of political resonance at that moment? Or is not the sharing of food with others a small social contract analogous to the contract of giving and taking—of interaction—that we call citizenship in a democratic society? Is this a stretch? Can we only be political when we are speaking to specific issues of identity, exclusion, injustice?

Resistance might be the one thing that governs what we think of as political. And in that light, I'd hardly call roasting a chicken a political act (unless perhaps I were to roast a chicken and serve it defiantly to my vegetarian friends . . .). But who determines what the things we choose to resist should be? We've heard the term "politically correct" forever, it seems. But increasingly there seems a push to be *correctly political*. How this translates is that there is a small group of things that we—by which I mean poets of outsiderness, of whatever kind—are expected to write from and about, and it comes down to an even smaller group of identity markers, race, gender, sexual orientation, as I've mentioned, when in fact there are so many aspects by which identity gets both established and recognized. This is in no way to say that the identity markers I've mentioned aren't immensely important; they just aren't solely important.

———

"What color are the people in your poems? You don't say."

———

How we write seems to me as valid a way of being political as what we choose to write *about*. Years ago, a poet friend suggested that I'd made a new kind of language, a new way of handling English, noticeable, he said, in my first book but consolidated in the second. I had no idea what he was talking about, but I did what I usually do when afraid of seeming clueless: I nodded with apparent understanding. It was through reviews that I learned the issue was syntax, that my sentences were inflected in ways likely traceable to a background in Greek and Latin. I had truly never considered this; my sentences are pretty much models of how I actually think, but it does seem reasonable that a way of thinking might be influenced by one's exposure to other ways of thinking, down to the level of the sentence. And, years before studying Greek and Latin, I'd lived in Germany for four years as a child and become fluent in German, itself a highly inflected language.

None of this is especially political in and of itself. But in the context of a contemporary poetry largely governed by the demotic use of language—that is, sentences that reflect how the majority of people in this country speak on a daily basis—a choice to use sentences that, in their inflectedness, sound *other* becomes a potentially political act. (In this case, it's interesting to think about how a syntax that is very old—not just in Western Europe, but also evident in the American sentences of Melville, Emerson, Henry James, all of them influenced by the Greco-Roman oratorical tradition—can seem suddenly radical, once the context, in terms of grammar and syntax, has shifted.) Add the context of my sexuality, and suddenly another way to put it is that I'm queering language and, by extension, the sentence itself. I think this queering of language can be political in at least a couple of ways, one more nuanced than the other. A writer can deliberately take the usual elements of language and force those elements to turn against, as it were, the traditions those elements have served, historically—the reason for doing so being to speak on behalf of those who have been oppressed by said tradition. At the level of form, Robert Hayden's deft fusing of the Negro spiritual, English hymn tradition, and blank verse to describe a slave mutiny and address racial oppression more broadly, in "Middle Passage," is a clear example. So is W. S. Merwin's rejection of the hierarchies that implicitly come with the use of punctuation. And so is Adrienne Rich's restless sifting through, reshaping of, and abandoning of prosodic forms across a career spent questing for a common language.

That is one way, then, to queer language—deliberately, and for the purpose of tailoring it to one's own purposes. The other is less intentional, and is the one I myself more relate to. I make sentences not to argue for outsiderness, but as the only space in which my outsiderness makes sense to me. From the start, I've thought of writing as a near-physical wrestling with all but unpindownable concerns. Though I may have been surprised by Hadas's introduction to my first book, I absolutely knew I was trying to make sense of my sexual self, and I seemed unable to get anything onto the page when I tried writing in the more straightforward style of the poets I admired at the time, William Carlos Williams, in particular, whose clarity was enviable to me. But that particular kind of clarity was not, I think, what I was ready for, in terms of thinking about being gay. And in this light, it makes sense to me that the sentences that made sense to me were on one hand the ones that felt most natural to me, but they also were sentences that would tell and not tell, ones that could possibly distract from what they were telling by telling it, as Emily Dickinson would say, slant. In a sense, I see this as the mind's way of rescuing; it allows the poet to process their sense of crisis, and to give voice to it, but in a way that spares having to directly face facts—as if the mind knew we might not yet be ready for that. I also see it as simply being how I write—which is to say, being who I am. It's also political.

———

"I liked it when you were still a gay poet," an audience member said to me at a Q and A, once, explaining that I seemed to have moved away from that after my second book. What he meant, I think, is that he preferred the queerness served without surprise or nuance. That book contains several overtly sexual scenes between men; there's the desire to flaunt sex itself as the main part of liberation—a desire appropriate, I'd say, to someone who's just come out, especially back in the early 1990s. I don't disavow those poems at all, but they don't reflect the maturity of thinking that comes after sex becomes understood as but an aspect—possibly the easiest to fathom— of an identity that's ever shifting as the contexts of age and experience shift in turn. Another way of putting it is that I'm gay when I'm having sex, sure; but I'm no less gay when I'm thinking about sex more abstractly.

———

Me: I'm having some difficulty understanding the intentions of your poem.

Male grad student: That's because when I write it's mainly for a male reader.

Me: Uh, excuse me, but I am male.

Male grad student: I mean like a *male* male reader.

———

The above exchange says many things, but the part I'm most interested in here is how some writers are deliberately writing toward a particular audience, how this works as a political act. To my mind, the point of writing is to communicate something to someone—by which I mean, to anyone who wants to read what I've written. By this logic, the choice to ignore one audience for another, to privilege a chosen audience, is highly political, inasmuch as it's a choice to refuse to risk compromising one's own stance or voice by engaging with an otherness on that otherness's terms. This is related to but different from Countee Cullen writing, for example, a Keatsian sonnet, a form that we could say invites a White reader in, but in terms of subject matter critiques the conditions imposed by a White readership. It's more like Langston Hughes's argument for turning to the daily language of the Harlem he knew, and employing that in poetry—doubly political, because on one hand rejecting an accepted "White" vernacular for a "Black" one, and on the other hand, in doing so, making an argument for Black vernacular as equivalent to, and therefore just as worthy of being poetry, as White vernacular. I think of the Black Arts Movement, as well, part of whose agenda was to write a poetry of immediacy, as in immediately accessible to an audience that might not ordinarily turn to poetry. This makes sense, when the point is to motivate a community toward effective and efficient action. Poetry that requires an MFA or a Ph.D. in philology isn't going to do the trick. Nuance is also not the best tool in this situation. Hence the clarity—necessarily blistering, at times—of that movement. (It's worth noting, as well, how those poems largely eschew punctuation and/or its traditional usage, what we've seen in Merwin, what we often see in L=A=N=G=U=A=G=E poetry and its various descendants—which is to say, it's interesting to see how the same political method crosses racial borders; radicalism is often a lot more democratic than we at first suppose.)

But what about the opposite of choosing which readers to write for? What if, by their mere being, our poems speak to an audience we hadn't *not* chosen, we simply hadn't intended the poems to resonate in a particular way, though resonance has everything to do with who's reading our work, and how? A poem of mine, "White Dog," has many things to say, I hope, but the basic situation of the poem is as unexciting as follows: a speaker walks his dog, who is white, in a snowstorm, and contemplates unleashing the dog even though he knows the dog—a female, incidentally—won't come back. At the Q and A afterward (I begin to see the Q and A as a concept itself fraught with potentially political resonance), an African-American woman asked me why the dog in the poem was white. I told her the truth—the dog I owned at the time was white. She seemed dissatisfied, and sat down. But she approached me again at the reception, and insisted that my poem was a critique of White women on the part of a Black man, the speaker presumably myself, in control (via the leash) of a Whiteness and femaleness that I then considered releasing—hence the poem considered Black male enslavement of and ultimate rejection of White femaleness.

"White Dog" is a poem ultimately about recognizing something about oneself that one would like to let go of, as a way of saving it from the less pleasant parts of a self. The woman at the reception had equated the speaker with myself; she'd missed the part in the poem where the speaker equates the dog with his *better* self. In some ways, I'm glad she missed that, since I can imagine a line of thinking by which I equate my better self with the dog's whiteness . . . from there to the anxieties of miscegenation . . . from there to madness . . .

And yet, it seems fair enough—and more to the point, beyond my control—if a reader brings their own concerns and lenses of experience to a poem and comes away with a reading different from, and more politically charged than, the one we'd intended. Fair enough, if the reading is extrapolated ultimately from what the poem itself provides. The dog's whiteness and femaleness are facts. Less so, the speaker's race or, for that matter, gender, since neither is specified in the poem. In a

sense, then, a reader's experience is the catalyst for reader
response, and that response can be the catalyst for the polit-
icization of a poem that was, otherwise, merely being itself.
Again, fair enough. Though vaguely troubling.

———

None of what I'm saying here is in any way meant to speak
against a more overtly political poetry or to deny its validity
or, indeed, its necessity. If anything, I'm arguing against too
narrow a definition of political. I know political has chiefly,
as a word, to do with governing—and usually more specifically the governing of an entity such as a nation, a body of
citizens, from the Greek *politikos,* relating to citizens, the people of the state, *polis* in Greek. But in these post-Emersonian,
post-Thoreauvian United States, there's surely room for the
idea of government of the self *by* the self. There's plenty that
we can't control in life, and merely being oneself is not always
a given—plenty of places, still, where to be open in certain
ways can mean ostracism, even death. But poetry is, in particular, so rooted in individual sensibility, it seems a shame if
we can't be free to express ourselves as we choose—or more
realistically, I think we have no real choice in the matter. A
reason to broaden the definition of political is that each individual is different, and our poems will necessarily reflect that.
In a democracy, that seems to me to mean that those who

must write as witness to the savagery of, say, war should do so—that's part of the record of what it means to be alive right now in the twenty-first century. So too, though, is the intimacy between a parent and child, so too is the agony of private despair that can displace, for a time, what also counts as part of life—joy, in its myriad forms. To be alive has never been one thing, any more than a period of history is. At the same time, people are complex creatures, and we manifest our sensibilities in many ways. Writing is just one of them. Which is to say, speaking for myself at least, my poems are simply how one aspect of my sensibility gets enacted; other parts might be manifest in how I dress, or interact with others, or by the hobbies I choose. Not everything gets written down, nor does it have to. We should no more make assumptions about who a person is, based on that person's poetry, than we should be assuming how they should write, and about what, based on who we think a person is.

———

To each his own urgency. Or hers. Or theirs. How is it not political, to be simply living one's life meaningfully, thoughtfully, which means variously in keeping with, in counterpoint to, and in resistance to life's many parts? To insist on being who we are is a political act—if only because we are individuals, and therefore inevitably resistant to society, at the very

least by our differences from it. If the political must be found
in differences of identity, who gets to determine which parts
of identity are the correct ones on which to focus? I write
from a self for whom race, gender, and sexual orientation are
never outside of consciousness—that would be impossible—
but they aren't always at the forefront of consciousness. Others write otherwise, as they must, as they should—as we all
should, if collectively we are to be an accurate reflection of
what it will have been like to have lived in this particular time
as our many and particular selves.

———

Here's a poem, "Cathedral," from my book *Double Shadow:*

> And suddenly—strangely—there was also no fear, either.
> As a horse in harness to what, inevitably, must break it.
> No torch; no lantern—and yet no hiddenness, now. No hiding.
> Leaves flew through where the wind sent them flying.

Is this a Black poem? A queer poem? Why or why not and
who says.

PRACTICE

When I was ten, I wanted to learn to play the clarinet and eventually join the school band. But (or And, or So—) my father found an affordable, used, kid-sized accordion, somehow found a tutor, and that, plus his moving the whole family to an air force base in Germany (where the accordion is beloved) for the next four years both solidified my commitment to the accordion and guaranteed my never having a place in any school band. (Do schools maybe now find a place for the random accordionist? Why not a little zydeco with your team spirit? Or a mashup between a march and a waltz—I can almost hear it ...)

Putting aside how much this likely explains so many parts of who I am today, I mean to say that from early on I associated practice with music; more exactly, practice meant the routine that might lead to mastery, whose proof would be my being able to play a piece all the way through without making mistakes. I got everything, as they say, wrong.

"Finally we forget what we are carrying and do not / make mistakes," says Pamela Alexander in the final two lines of her poem "The Vanishing Point." For me, these lines speak to what's truer, more realistic than mastery, namely, fluency. To be absolutely up front about it: I don't believe in mastery, when it comes to art, any more than I do when it comes to a relationship with another person. In both instances, the relationship—between two people, between art and maker—is symbiotic and organic, ever changing, on both sides, so how can there ever be mastery of what by definition never loses the ability to surprise, to change in ways that we can't predict? This is why I've always described a writing career as a lifelong apprenticeship to what can never be fully mastered, even as the artistic impulse is an impulse *toward* mastery— that is, toward what only exists abstractly. In this way, I've also compared writing to devotion or prayer, both of which require absolute commitment to what can't be proven to exist; the commitment (or faith, to continue the analogy) "merely" proves that we *believe* something exists. But the commitment is everything.

Back to fluency, then, and practice. The point of practice is to repeat an action enough times that it becomes routine, which is to say "we forget what we are carrying," to return to Alexander's poem, which links this forgetting directly to no longer making mistakes. By this logic, mistakes are the result of being overly aware of what we're doing; once we lose this awareness, something else—I'll call it instinct, intuition—takes over, a separate part of the mind, presumably. It's as if we can think now without thinking about thinking—that is, without making mistakes, without interrupting our thoughts with doubt, or pride, or comparison with others, or concerns about audience, no fear . . .

Many years ago, having studied Italian for a few years, having been pronounced officially fluent, I went to study in Rome for a summer. And indeed, everywhere I went, I could understand what I heard, and could convey my own thoughts in turn. But each time I said anything in Italian, I had to mentally "set it up" in English first, recall the Italian, then speak; likewise, I'd consciously translate each sentence I heard from others. Then a couple of weeks into my stay, I woke from a dream and realized that the entire dream had been in Italian, and that I'd been speaking and listening to Italian not as translated but as instinctively understood. And for the rest of my summer there, I no more thought about speaking Italian than I did about speaking English. I simply spoke. At last, I was fluent.

I couldn't have reached that fluency, though, without the constant repetition and memorization of vocabulary, rules of grammar, nuances of syntax and intonation. Likewise, to practice writing, before fluency, means writing something on a regular basis. This can take many forms, and will vary from person to person. Here, by the way, I think it's more important not to have art as the absolute goal, or even the goal at all. It's too intimidating. In this regard, though I've never myself been one to keep a journal, a journal is definitely a good way of committing to a routine practice of putting words on a page. As I understand it, journaling just means recording our thoughts at the time, whatever highlights of a given day, the weather. The point here is a physical and mental engagement with the act of writing, until the joining of thought and writing becomes instinctive, and in turn to write becomes conducive to thinking, becomes both a catalyst for curiosity and the medium by which curiosity extends itself like light—but somehow more physical than light—into the so-called darkness of what's yet to be stumbled upon, what we call discovery.

A different form of practice—of routinely filling a blank page or screen with language—is imitation, which can take many forms. Often, I'll try imitating a poem's structure; I'll admire a fifteen-line poem that's written in five three-line stanzas, where each line has no more than six words in it. Again, I'm not trying to write a poem, I'm trying to fill an existing form—

in this case, I'm also practicing stanza-length and line-length. Or I'll choose a random paragraph in a novel, count how many sentences it consists of, and then write that many sentences as a paragraph of my own. Or I'll learn a new word on social media: just a couple of days ago, it was "wintercearig"; I saw it on Twitter, and it apparently means something like winter sorrow, or maybe more broadly a sorrow resulting from the accumulation of years in a life. In my early years of trying to write—still practicing toward fluency—I'd have written wintercearig ten times in a row in my notebook, as a way to remember it, and to possibly use it in future, but mainly again as a way of engaging with the act of writing.

———

I don't mean to suggest that once we've attained fluency we never make mistakes, and each line is perfect. Going back to Alexander, I think she means the one specific mistake of being overly self-conscious of what we are physically doing. I feel I'm able to write more freely, more daringly, because I'm not hampered by thoughts like Is this a poem that I'm writing; Am I even a writer; Will anyone read this and, if they do, will they like it; Does it make sense; What if . . . For me the act of writing is a quest of imagination, and the point is to risk the unknown, to become lost without worrying about it, without wondering how I'll get home; this is much likelier to happen if

I don't think too hard about where I'm going, or why. And it's especially more likely if I forget *how* I'm getting there, namely, my hand on this pen right now, inching it across the page of this notebook toward something like a chapter for a book whose deadline is only months from now . . . And just like that, I've thrown myself off—first the trail, now my horse—

To begin again: fluency doesn't mean we don't make any mistakes at all. But the mistakes we end up making are more likely to be the useful kind (in which case, is "mistake" the right word in the end?), steps, casts of mind, that aren't the usual ones, that suggest something about and to ourselves that we hadn't considered before, the possibility for discovery that I mentioned earlier, which is one of the most essential tools for warding off redundancy, for still having something new to say and (maybe more important, when it comes to sustaining a commitment to writing over many years—a lifetime) yet another new way of saying what we've said before. Those useful mistakes get the words on the page—footprints, as it were, as the mind staggers forward. But of course, once I have a draft, I can see that in my having wandered I misspelled a word here and there, or I chose the wrong word, or I can hear now, as I read a particular few lines aloud, that the sameness of pattern means I need to rough up the rhythm a bit, or—very common, for me—there's a whole chunk of what I've written that is not only outside of what the poem wants to talk about, but it's badly written. I remove that part, grateful for it though, since I clearly needed to write it in order to get to the next handful of lines, without which I'd have no poem. (I note, now, that how Alexander breaks her line means her poem's final line is "make mistakes," which can be read as an imperative—that mistakes should be made; they might ruin the original "plan," but they might equally lead to something better, that we never thought to plan . . .)

So, fluency doesn't displace the need for revision. It allows instead for the useful "mistakes" that are like the stepping-stones of imagination. Revision's a kind of cleaning up of my idiosyncratic path. The poem is something less idiosyncratic and, with luck, more useful; the poem is a map, but after the fact: not a way of getting somewhere, but a record of having been lost, of where that lostness brought me, until what was uncharted country became, for the space of the poem, a place to live.

———

Meanwhile, having attained fluency also doesn't mean that we can now sit down and write whenever we feel like it, summoning it as if on command. This brings me to another sense of the word "practice," one that has only become a point of discussion fairly late in my teaching life. More and more, I'm asked by students to meet with them in order to help them establish a "writing practice" for themselves. I didn't know what this meant, the first time, but I soon gathered that a writing practice is a way of structuring a life to incorporate and be conducive to one's writing, at once an ongoing sort of self-education, a carving-out of time within which to write, and a means of creating readiness for or receptivity to the next idea worth giving voice to. I also gathered that my students had assumed I must already have such a practice in place myself, though my own way of proceeding as a writer is mostly patternless, it feels that way, and yet . . .

My initial impulse was to tell my students simply to write, to make a point of reading, to practice as I've described above. Their questions went beyond this, however, and were more urgent: When, and how often, and for how long, and where? As I once asked, in another context, in a poem, Which way's the right way? Part of me wants to say that artists never ask for permission to proceed in whatever way they have to. But that's more easily said than done. We want to be ourselves, but we want to know we're being ourselves in the "right" way, which is to say we want confirmation of both things, incongruously: that we are the unique artist we need to be, and that we are deemed an artist by others—that we *belong.* Not even the most "original" writers, that I can think of, have managed to avoid this dilemma entirely.

Establishing a writing practice depends equally on personal temperament and one's daily life apart from writing, which is to say—for most of us—most of daily life. How a full-time student might set up a writing practice is very different from how, for example, a parent with three children at home might do so. Or someone, say, whose chronic illness necessarily affects not just the patterns but the available energy of each day. Maybe the first step, then, in establishing a practice is to clearly assess how one's daily life is structured already—which parts are fixed, and which are flexible?

I was teaching high school full time when I began writing the poems that would become my first book. With the exception of summer break, that meant being at school by 6:45 each weekday morning and not getting home until about 3, when I'd spend the next couple of hours grading homework to be returned the next day. I was also married, the two of us making just enough money to cover the essentials of rent, utilities, and groceries, which meant that once we'd both returned home from work we'd cook dinner from scratch; then the catching up with each other, our respective days . . . And then it was evening, with maybe four hours before going to bed early enough to get up at 5 the next morning. Writing was the last thing I felt capable of, after work and dinner, so I spent those four evening hours reading: some poetry, but mostly all the novels I felt remiss in not having read before (though I was only, what, 24, 25?), *Middlemarch, Anna Karenina,* most of Dickens, Henry James, and Proust, with the odd bit of nonfiction from Jung and Freud, William James, Joseph Campbell. It all seems, as I look back on it, a pretty random assortment, but I can see now exactly how each of these has shaped my own writing, even as the routine of reading each night has continued to inform my daily life; which is to say, I was already establishing for myself a writing practice without thinking to do so. For me, a key part of writing is to read good writing, to see how others have done it. My daily life back then allowed only four hours of free time on weekdays; I've never been much of a fan of television, and reading books from the library was free, which aligned perfectly with my having no money to go anywhere. This is what I mean by developing a practice around temperament and what's actually possible, time-wise, after accounting for the fixed responsibilities of a job, a relationship, the need to eat.

As for actual writing, I was more deliberate; I decided that Sunday morning would be my writing time. Saturday was for chores—groceries, the laundromat—and Sunday afternoon was for writing out the week's lesson plans and ironing the week's work clothes (I used to iron . . .). That left Sunday morning, which I'd begin at 5 (a habit already, given teaching), working til noon. Sometimes I'd write a poem; more often I'd do imitations, as mentioned earlier. I remember a winter of working my way slowly through John Hollander's prosody book *Rhyme's Reason,* teaching myself each form by writing two examples of each form in the book. I knew no poets, I had no teachers to tell me what to read or when to write, so I read what I thought I both needed and wanted to read, and I wrote when I could. Which is to say, a writing practice includes not only writing and reading, but the discipline as well, to maintain a commitment to writing and reading, for which there's no magic recipe. If anything, I'd say the only real catalyst for discipline is a desire for what discipline can lead to. It's been said before, of course, but if you really must write, you'll find the discipline required to do so.

Reading, writing, discipline—is that it, then? I've left for last the most important and obvious yet most often overlooked or underestimated part of any writing practice: living one's life attentively. Any poem I write is at some level both a record and an enactment of what it means to live inside a human body for a particular few moments in time. It's as much an arc of thinking as of sensation. Not only is everything I experience— even the most seemingly negligible thing—potential subject matter for the next poem, but I experience each moment through the steadily accumulating lenses of everything I've ever experienced before. Which means that our lives themselves are both research for the next poem and the medium by which we conduct that research. An easier way of putting it is that poems don't get written by spending one's time exclusively in books, in front of blank screens and pages; it's crucial to get out into the world, to experience it as fully as possible, and to pay attention to that experience. Doing so is also a useful distraction from the frustration of not being able to write, or to write well. So in addition to reading and trying to write, both in a disciplined way, I also make a point each day of going for walks (a dog helps). I'm also the one who cooks in the family—cooking counts. Or the weather's too lousy and I don't feel like cooking, so I look for a steady few minutes at the weather from my window, or I close my eyes and listen to the weather that, when I can't see it, actually has its own music, not so lousy after all, I hadn't noticed, how hadn't I noticed this before? This doesn't mean my next poem will concern weather or putting a Bolognese sauce together or the bark of a tree that I noticed while walking, but these all get added to the countless things I've noticed, smelled, listened to across a longish life and they leave a for-the-most-part-untraceable imprint on each thought and gesture that follows, including the thought-and-gesture work of poems.

To get away from the reading and writing can also lead to problem solving, when it comes to the writing. Often when I can't come up with a title or when I can tell the writing's not as it should be, but I can't tell how or how to fix it, I'll go for a walk or vacuum a room or start some laundry. At the very least, I feel I've done something productive to counter the feeling of having wasted my time with a bad draft. But often, the change of activity also shakes me loose—distracts me—from the thinking I was stuck in: the bad draft suddenly has potential, I can see now what's missing or where I strayed from the point or what I meant to say all along. Activity, then, of any kind, according to our own individual abilities and circumstances, is not just research, not just distraction, but often clarifying, a form of revision, in fact, the many selves through which we experience the world have been ever-so-slightly recalibrated, we return to the writing changed, what looked like failure, a waste of time, seems also changed; now it looks like possibility.

Writing is intuitive, personal, private, and must ultimately be self-directed. So too with a writing practice, which can maybe be likened to the invisible shapes we each leave in the air behind us as we move from one space to the next one. Those shapes are unique to each of us. There's no right or wrong shape—just our own. Or maybe the air that contains those shapes is analogous to a writing practice, the context within and from which we leave behind us these records—the writing, that is—of having been here. Who can say?

To shape for oneself a writing practice is to commit to an apprenticeship in readiness. In order to write, we need to be ready to write, which means being informed, curious, fluent, patient, disciplined, and open to possibility however strange or sometimes frightening or perhaps at first not even worth writing about. The task, remember, is not transcription, but transformation. Little choir. "In this blue light, I can take you there," says Jorie Graham. And as if in response, there's Rilke: "You must change your life." I say: our lives change anyway. Pay attention; practice. Do it again. I sat down to write the conclusion of this essay in the winter 5 a.m. darkness. It's day now. The scattered oaks that punctuate the pines that gird the house are leafless except for one, a condition there's a name for that I can't remember right now, though I looked it up yesterday. There's a kind of brightness to the morning where you realize this is likely as bright as the day will get.

AUDIENCE

My partner's upstairs, still asleep. My dog is snoring on the sofa across the room from me. Outside it is 7 degrees and the phone says it feels like −6. I believe the phone. On it, or through it, or across the screen where paper used to be, for the writing of letters, a friend in Utah tells me he's been doing some catch-and-release fishing, which his girlfriend calls cruel. He tells me the fish only get hooked through the lip, so "it's only a little cruel," he says, and I surprise myself by agreeing, accepting cruelty as a fact and hierarchical, rather than arguing that our chief duty as human beings is to abstain from cruelty, less because we should (though I believe we should) than because we can. This guy is a national forest firefighter who also makes beautiful pots and bowls and mugs, as sturdy as they are also somehow tender—a lot like their maker, I suspect—which makes me wonder who any of us are. And what. And why.

What is the difference between the story we tell of ourselves to others and the song of ourselves that we keep private and sing to nobody else?

Sometimes I think I write to remind myself of what's been inside me all along, that I hadn't noticed or just forgot at some point and then, remembering, just assumed was lost. But that's not right, any of it. "It's a human need, / to give to shapelessness / a form," is how I put it in a poem once. To be more specific about the shapelessness, I think the catalysts for making poems—any art, really—come down to two: all the ideas, memories, desires that we can't let go of, what I call obsessions; and the other (though they are sometimes the same) ideas, memories, desires that won't let *us* go, what I usually call demons, though they're more properly familiars, for they're not always evil in their intent, nor are they always entirely unwelcome, sometimes, even if inconvenient. In writing a poem, I'm mapping the simultaneous distance and intimacy between my obsessions and my demons. And it's as if, having mapped this, I briefly know where I am, how I got here, and when I'm lost, as I surely will be, how to get back home. Poems aren't the only way of mapping and giving context to the emotional and psychological interior. For my friend in Utah, it's making pottery—and maybe fishing, too.

Or, to put it otherwise:

A way of
crossing a dark so unspecific, it seems
everywhere: isn't that what singing, once,
was for?

Yes, if by singing can also be meant the making of poems or any other art; and if by the unspecific dark can be meant whatever uniquely and relentlessly disturbs us into needing to give shape to it, be it large and external—war, prejudice, corporate indifference to individual suffering—or what feels sometimes smaller and more internal—desire and the fact of it, best intentions and the routine inability (failure?) to follow through on them, the likely reality (I'm pretty certain) that none of it will have mattered, we stop moving, forever . . . Which is to say, art begins as private and interior and utilitarian insofar as it's a way to arrange thought into a shape that, in articulating that thought, makes thought communicable—to whom, though?

First, to ourselves, I think. That's at least been my own experience. I long ago described poems as advance bulletins from the interior, for the way that poems often seem ahead of us in giving voice to what we aren't yet ready to hear, what the mind seems—as if mercifully—to protect us from hearing, *until* we're ready. We are, each one of us, many selves simultaneously coinciding and refusing to. The self that can provide—through articulated thought—a way through conundrum addresses that other self that can't find, or has lost, the way. The queer self that I couldn't yet acknowledge, let alone love, was my first audience. I sang myself through, or more exactly, one of my selves sang another one through. Those songs became my first book.

This idea of the self as first audience isn't limited, by the way, to writing that's primarily about personal identity and interiority. Even writers who from the start want to address a public audience about a public concern like, for example, police brutality, first have to figure out their personal stake in the issue (why this issue and not another) as well as their personal take on it (how do they differently understand it), as well, too, as their unique way of communicating this understanding to an audience that, whether it knows it yet or not, will be better off (so the writer believes—has to) for having finally received it.

And yet it's also the case that, whenever I'm asked whom I'm writing to, or for, I routinely answer that I don't think about audience. I guess what I mean is that I don't think—not while writing—past myself as the addressee. Even in poems where I address a you—if it's not myself, if it's (as is often the case) the other person in a relationship that we share together, then it's my private idea of that person as I get to force them to be, through imagination: patiently listening without interrupting me, easily persuaded, until at last they believe what I believe, that what I've said is true. That's how I feel, at least, when I've finished a poem: that in saying a thing, I've made it briefly so . . . Whether or not, though, others need to hear it, I initially write whatever *I* need to hear. I think most writers do. Even Langston Hughes, when he addresses America. Even Frank O'Hara, justifying his errant ways to the harbormaster. Even Hopkins when, in what looks like despair, he cries out to God.

But any art that lasts must eventually resonate with others beyond the maker's self. Of course, when I write I don't think that I'm writing poems that will last; I'm writing because that's how I make sense of my life, that's all. I don't think I could write if I thought of an audience—even one person— actually listening; it would intimidate me from being as honest and direct as I need to be in my attempts to interrogate and put to rest, for a time, what I feel overwhelmed by. Once we've decided, though, to share what we've made, there's an audience, one that we can only partially—and even then, sometimes barely—control.

We say what we say; that doesn't mean others will understand it or, if they do, that they won't dislike it. I learned this pretty quickly, at the first reading I ever gave from my first book. There were at most ten people in the bookstore audience, a handful of friends and a few strangers who didn't seem to have come for a reading but sat down out of curiosity. I began reading, and at my mention of a man's ass in the first poem, someone got up and left in what looked to me like outrage. Everyone else stayed through the reading, but looked increasingly nonplussed. "I'm reading about sex and tenderness and regret," I thought to myself—"doesn't everyone think about these things?" The answer even now, but especially then, in 1992, is no, or not quite so openly, or not in the context of two men. I somewhere understood that a desired effect of poetry was to disturb the reader from complacency, from their assumptions about a given subject—to counter those assumptions with a different "take." But what I couldn't have guessed was the forms, over the years, that an audience's reaction to being disturbed could take: from a feeling of kinship to sheer disgust, the poems getting labeled variously, from provocative and illuminating to shocking and even pornographic.

Writing doesn't require an audience beyond oneself and/or whatever audience one chooses to privately imagine. Art isn't any less—or more—as a result of being made public, be it via performance, whatever forms of social media, appearance in print, or even just showing what we've made to a friend. "The Soul selects her own Society," says Dickinson, and sometimes that society not only can be a society of one—the self—but maybe *should* be. Not only can keeping your art to yourself allow for the simple pleasure of having made a thing, without any outside opinions as to the relative and always subjective value of what you've made; it also allows you to write—and to grow *into* writing—as your unique sensibility needs to, what some call finding your own voice, but I think of it more as coming into a clearer understanding of how your particular accumulation of experiences as a body continuing to move across a life enacts and commemorates those experiences, both bodily and intellectually, in the form of making, in all its variousness: mistakes, decisions, art, small gestures . . . Ultimately, I'm grateful that I sort of stumbled into writing and that I wrote for years without any awareness that poetry could be something more than a private hobby. Of course I knew there were poetry books, written by people still living, but I had no idea that writing programs existed, that there were degrees to be had, that some people not only got paid to teach poetry but to merely recite it for a half hour or so—what? Likewise, I had no notion of what might be "appropriate" in terms of subject matter and ways of expressing it. As a result, I wrote what I needed to, in the *way* that I needed to—not out of willfulness, superiority, or anything like bravery, but out of an assumption that this must be how everyone writes, in the fruitful absence of anyone bothering to take notice, which is to say, in the complete freedom from audience.

Hard to say how technology will have changed even a year, never mind ten years, from now, if anyone then should read this. But social media of some kind is likely to be around, still, as long as there are people who wish to communicate with each other. The idea of cultivating an audience is hardly a new phenomenon—the oral tradition that includes such works as the *Iliad* and the *Koran* is shaped around harnessing and sustaining an audience's attention; but social media, in the form of likes and numbers of followers, certainly amplifies not only the idea of cultivating an audience in measurable terms, but the idea as well that value itself—quality—can be measured, and that audience response is the objective gauge to measure it by. It is not, if only because audiences consist of human beings who, among other limitations, can never be entirely objective.

I've written earlier in these pages about the pitfalls of confusing the attention of audience with love. Perhaps it's best to treat audience as love itself is best treated: being loved by someone gives me another perspective on life, it shouldn't eclipse or erase my own. I hope to learn from those who love me—to be nurtured toward my best self, who I *am* and *can* be, not pressured by expectation into what others have decided I *should* be. I've also written of how audience can interpret and politicize our writing in ways that don't reflect what we even remotely intended to say, but which conform exactly to what the listener or reader instead needed—or preferred—to hear. Isn't this, too, like what often passes for love?

AUDIENCE

As when, though you continue to live with and make a home with another person—but as if you were sometimes strangers to each other—you can't decide if you no longer love them or if it's possible that you've just forgotten you still do: either way, a muddle.

Misinterpretations are not the same, though, as alternative interpretations we may not have intended but are no less reasonable, despite that. Which is to say, our poems can have applications in contexts we can't imagine and, therefore, can't anticipate. In "A Mathematics of Breathing," a poem from my second book, I was trying to write about patience, I think, about taking a breath at a time, instructions to myself, really, having just come out as gay, having just begun my first relationship with another man; everything was happening so quickly, I needed to remind myself: take your time. But about a decade later, Madge McKeithen recounted in her book *Blue Peninsula: Essential Words for a Life of Loss and Change* how she found words in my poem that she could apply to and find helpful for contextualizing her son's sudden, undiagnosable illness, as she navigated the journey, as a mother, through her son's steady decline and eventual death. The she at the end of my poem is Scheherazade from *One Thousand and One Nights,* but it could as easily be McKeithen, writing her book:

When she tells her own story,

Breathe in,
breathe out

is how it starts.

Years after having written my poem, I met McKeithen at a book signing after a reading I'd given, and we spoke briefly about the serendipity of when and how we encounter a stranger's work, the different uses—different lives, really—that our work gets to have for others once we've released it. I'm still grateful for that opportunity to have proof of this lucky phenomenon. More often, we have no idea how our work has affected or been of use to others—this is true enough while we're alive, but absolutely true once we're not. The nineteenth-century poet John Clare could never have anticipated that a Black teenager in the 1970s would come across an illustrated version of Clare's poem "The Badger" while shelving books at his afterschool library job. Having been bullied through most of school—for being Black, an enthusiastic smart nerd, useless at sports, and with no sign of a "normal" interest in girls—I took strange comfort in Clare's portrait of the badger's resilience in the face of torture from schoolboys and adults alike; yes, the badger dies in the end, but he does so heroically—this was not nothing. Nor was it nothing for me to consider, thanks to Clare's poem, the apparent timelessness of being singled out and punished for not fitting in; there was a value, then, in being stubbornly oneself, even if it might not save you. The poem itself seemed proof of the value of that stubbornness, that someone thought to commemorate the badger's life and death in a poem. Again, not nothing.

As I tell my students, and routinely remind myself as well, once we choose to release what we've made into the world— again, in whatever form, a particular friend or a packed lecture hall, on a stage or in the local newspaper—we lose control of it. This being the case, what begins to matter most, I think, is the spirit with which, if we choose to, we share our art. I can't deny that when I first started sending poems to magazines and eventually took a first workshop—my first time ever showing poems to a group of people who actually thought of themselves as poets (!)—I definitely hoped for confirmation that my poems were good, that I wasn't wrong in imagining I had something worth saying. That's human enough. But as I've said, it took just one public reading for me to understand how random and unpredictable in its responses an audience can be. Since then, as with my teaching, when I share my work I do so in the spirit simultaneously of generosity and what I call an invitation to instruction. Here is something I've written, from who I am, deep down, as a flawed human being trying to navigate and make sense of what, for as long as it lasts, keeps changing: life itself, my one small eventually-to-be-forgotten example of it, in the shape of this poem—here, it's yours if you want it, and if there's something useful for you, that you can learn from, that's yours too; and if there isn't, well, deciding what we don't like or can find no use for is also essential, as much to shaping personal taste as to revising, recalibrating, and clarifying who we are as individuals in relationship to a world of others. That world is vast. Our lives, though finite, are likewise vast, have vastnesses inside them. In encountering the art of others, I learn how others have differently negotiated these vastnesses—they resonate with me or don't, depending. Likewise, my poems are the proof of my own negotiations—both the tools with which I made a small opening, and the means by which I moved forward, through that opening. "Let us / make of what's left a sturdiness we can use to the end." Whether others will find what I've left behind useful for themselves is neither within my control nor has it ever even been my wish exactly *to* control it. I wanted to live; I wrote; I did what I had to.

COMMUNITY

I once heard a writer argue against figurative language—simile, especially—because of its implications about power. The argument seemed to be that simile, in suggesting that one thing is like another, suggests as well the equation of some things, therefore the *un*equal-ness of other things, which is to say that not all things are equal; once value is introduced, so is power; simile, by this argument, becomes an insidious way for language to create and reinforce a system of unfairness, of power and the unfair distribution of it. I get that argument, and, without dismissing it at all, I disagree with it.

At the level of animal instinct, the ability to recognize likeness is a survival tool. It's the way—or a chief way—in which we grapple with the potential danger that strangeness always, at first, equals. If we don't know what a thing is, we don't know if it's safe or threatening. The example I often turn to is an encounter with something in my path while walking through the woods. Something slightly twisted in shape, and motionless. I can't tell from this distance, but as I get closer it seems it could be a snake—that is, it looks possibly like a snake, which is to say I've engaged in simile. If it is a snake, the motionlessness suggests it might be a dead snake—in which case, no threat ... I get closer, and I realize it looks more like a twisted, leafless branch (another simile), which turns out to be the case. In this way, simile—thinking via figurative language— becomes the way in which I narrow possibilities down in order to identify what may or may not be safe. All of this happens in the brain within seconds, as I understand it, the mind sifting quickly through what it knows via the senses—what does this strange thing look like, sound like, smell like? (This is why, by the way, to be an artist of any originality at all is to be held suspect, at first; for such artists, sustaining a career in which their art finds outside acceptance means waiting, on the one hand, for the rest of the world to learn how to acknowledge that art *as* art, by watching it long enough to recognize it as familiar; and on the other hand, it means remembering that to grow as an artist is to keep changing—to surprise, which means routinely defamiliarizing and disrupting expectation. No easy task!)

But it's also true that the most powerful similes don't so much equate like with like as suggest equation where it's not immediately apparent; in doing so, similes have the potential to integrate—to invite an openness to diversity, by provoking readers to simultaneously revise their assumed understanding of the world and to include within it—as a valid, valued part of it—perceived difference. The understanding of likeness and of how different doesn't have to mean unrecognizable and therefore dangerous is a prerequisite for compassion, without which, within a human society of many individuals—which is to say, a community of restless, ever-shifting points of agreement and disagreement—there would be no peace.

Meanwhile, though, to risk asking a likely tinderbox of a question: what's so wrong, inherently at least, with value? I don't mean to ignore a long history of people using value to justify atrocity—money, over human decency, for example, one race above another, all the damage done—emotionally, physically, psychologically—by media-driven and -imposed standards of beauty, et cetera. But, like anyone, I care more about some things than about other things. I prefer a wild yard to a manicured one; books mean more to me than sports; I'd rather live in the woods than in a city; I dislike tapioca.

When I say we are not the same, I mean we're individuals, individual in our tastes, ambitions, disappointments; we carry inside us our own wildernesses, as particular in their obsessions as they are various in their surprises. These differences give context to the points of likeness between us; or—to go further—likeness and difference require one another, the way shadow and light do. Or like love, and its absence.

———

The subject of community comes up a lot among writers. The idea seems to be that because we are all writers (or substitute here any form of making), we have even more than that in common, we share a mutual respect and empathy for each others' work, and we are there for each other, as a support system, for when we flounder in doubt, as we each sometimes do—as we must. But in its origins the word "community" itself has to do mostly with shared physical space, and a community consists of people who have in common the buildings they've erected, from the Latin *munio,* to build or fortify. This latter idea of fortifying does seem a likely link to thinking of community as a form of support, *for* a group from *within* that group. But with the professionalization of the writing community has come the idea that such a community is required, even as an advanced degree increasingly can seem to be required to be an artist, when it is not. If I could impart to my students only one thing, it would be that there is no single right way to do any of this business of making a life as a writer. How can there be— why should there be—given differences in individual temper-

ament and, when it comes to community, the different ways
to define and think of it?

Given, too, our different experiences of community, which
inevitably shape our relationship to it. Having grown up on
various air force bases until age thirteen, I came to think of
community as ever-changing and unpredictable, and therefore not to be relied upon. I'd make friends with a group of
kids, only to move—or learn that *they* had moved—halfway
through the school year. As a result, I quickly—subconsciously—revised community to mean the characters and
the worlds they inhabited in the books that I kept with me
each time my family moved. Which is to say, I still think of
community, even now, primarily as whatever can provide
reliable company, which has mostly meant things other than
actual people: books and their characters, animals wild and
domesticated, trees—maybe trees especially . . . This understanding of community isn't anything like, presumably, that of
the adult versions of those kids I met when my father retired
and we moved permanently to Massachusetts, where I began
high school, the first school I ended up attending all the way
through. These kids had gone to school together since kinder-
garten. For them, community meant sharers of a space that
had remained constant, as had their friendships, and feuds.
That difference between us in understanding only reinforced
in me my sense of outsiderness and the notion that when it

came to people, community meant a sharing merely of space, and only potentially—not inevitably—of sensibility. There are negatives to this way of thinking (I'm not the best at collaboration; trusting others isn't the most well-honed of my instincts), but the main advantage has been that working in solitude, without a community of fellow artists, has always felt right to me. Yes, when—as a high school teacher in a small town where I knew no writers—I first began writing, there was no other choice (that I knew of) but to work alone; but now that I do know plenty of writers to whom I could turn for guidance when stuck or for reassurance when wrestling with doubt (in myself, in the writing), I find I still choose to work through those periods alone—so I must prefer it.

Mostly.

It's hard to say, though, how much of this has to do with how I came to think of community through my experience with it, growing up, and how much is just sensibility: I'm an introvert. Others aren't. But whether I've always been this way or I've learned to be, or I was forced to be by most of the time not being included—for all kinds of reasons, including just being the new kid arriving in the middle of the school year—it scarcely matters now. Why explain, if for each explanation there's a contradiction? As a high school Latin teacher, I was mostly a party of one. Sure, I was part of a community of teachers, but usually the only Latin teacher, and my subject matter made me the odd-person-out, the teacher who was asked more than once to explain to the school board why Latin was relevant enough to justify their renewing my contract. What sustained me over the years was my membership in CANE, the Classical Association of New England, which I'd joined more out of duty than interest, initially. Membership meant receiving an occasional newsletter, and being invited to attend the annual conference. Bringing my usual skepticism with me, I attended my first conference, and felt immediately changed: who knew there were so many others for whom nerding out over the use of clauses in Caesar's *Commentaries* was fairly routine? As well as our interests, our situation— teaching a "dead" language, having to prove how and why it mattered—was also a bond. I felt more than included—welcomed; I didn't feel alone; what I realized was how lonely I'd sometimes felt but had assumed was just part of how it felt to be me. The conference lasted for a single weekend each year, but what I brought away with me sustained me through the rest of the year, and made it easier to push through doubt and occasional defeat.

So, too, with a writing workshop, as I eventually found out. It's true that I've often been grateful for having worked for years in the dark as a poet. Knowing no poets, and nothing at all about the existence of a "poetry world," I had to find

whatever a "voice" is on my own, and instead of being given a
reading list, had to shape my own from whatever I stumbled
upon in the library or a used bookstore. Not knowing there
were "rules" or "trends," I wrote whatever—and however—I
needed to. But somewhere in there I must have had doubts or
wanted some sort of confirmation, because the first time that
I showed a poem to a workshop—taught by Alan Dugan on
a pay-per-session basis at the Castle Hill Center for the Arts
in Truro, Massachusetts—the group's unanimous recognition
that what I'd shared with them was not just a poem but a good
one showed me that what I was doing meant something to
others besides myself: had resonance, though what I called
it at the time—erroneously, I think—was value. Or my error
was in thinking the poem hadn't had value until given such by
a group of readers, when the poem had meant something to
myself already—that should have been enough. Right?

It should be enough, and it is, but I'll admit I often have to
remind myself of this, even now.

Community often determines value; that doesn't mean it
should. But for all my introvertedness, I can't underestimate
the value of community itself. In the course of those summer weeks in workshop with Dugan, I learned to take my
work more seriously, to think about it critically; I learned the
strange usefulness of conflicting feedback; and maybe most

important, I learned that an impulse to make meaning with words in lines and stanzas might feel isolating, at times, but (as with being a Latin teacher) I'd never been alone. Meanwhile, who can say how things would be different if I'd continued to practice writing as a private hobby? There'd have been nothing "wrong" about that, at all. But it's through my poems that I came to understand and speak openly of my queerness (more openly than I realized, at the time), and the workshop, in reading and speaking of my poems with no judgment as to their content, quite literally provided a safe space in which I not only came to take myself seriously as a writer (it was the workshop that suggested I send poems to journals, and which ones; it was Dugan who urged me to assemble a manuscript and submit it to a contest), but to step into an embrace of who I was and am, as a gay man. As confused as I was about sexuality, and as suicidal as I'd sometimes felt in the face of that confusion, I've said that writing my poems saved my life; but if so, that small community of a poetry workshop for two summers did its own share of saving me. I see that now. How do I assign a value to that?

I don't mean, though, to reduce community to a tool by which to navigate an identity crisis or a gauge by which to determine the legitimacy of one's art. Community was, for a time, essential to me in those particular ways, but I think the larger importance of a writing community, at best, is as an ongoing reminder of likeness: not that we makers of meaning are interchangeable, in any way the same, but that we *share* something. This isn't the likeness that I started off talking about— the likeness of equation that implies the lack of it, that implies power and the distribution of it, which had made the writer whom I mentioned dismiss simile—but a likeness centered in an understanding that we share a vocation, a passion; likeness, then, as a system of exchanged support, community—again, at best—as a space of generosity, which can take many forms, including just being there, like taking another's hand in one's own for a time, and holding it, no words required. I think the best communities don't just provide support but include, too, an understanding that support works in both directions, and that those who choose to be part of a community won't just receive but give support back, not as a duty but as unforced and instinctive—as respect and compassion should be—as love itself.

Not every community, though, is the right one for a given person or at a given time. Dugan's workshop was right for me for a brief period during which I struggled to come out as a poet and a gay man. And I like to believe that, in offering support and constructive critique of my peers' work, I gave something useful back. I had a very different experience shortly after this, when I was asked to join—and was ousted from, about six months later—the Dark Room Collective, a group that had been established as a space for Black voices in a place (Cambridge, Massachusetts, at the time) dominated by a White establishment that had historically tried to keep all others out. I wasn't officially kicked out of the Dark Room; I'd say it was more that I was informed that I wasn't welcome, and—this is a little fuzzier to pin down, but I felt it—the reason was that I wasn't writing the kind of poems that were correctly "Black." I'd wrongly made the assumption, as they had, that having color in common would mean we saw the world, and more specifically our craft and aesthetic, the same way, or that we'd have every cause in common. That's naïve, maybe, but not a crime. We're individuals, we have different views, and sometimes those differences, though we should do our best, I think, to respect them, mean we can't get along. I don't find that unreasonable. Isn't that why, within a world of people all around us (a community of human beings, of fellow citizens within that, of shared identities and interests within that) we end up with the relatively small group of friends we do, whom we need, and want to love, who feel they can turn to us when *they're* in need, who can love us back?

It's important, then, to think carefully about community, and to choose wisely. Community can have an isolating effect, especially if how you proceed in the world doesn't comfortably square with how the community believes you should. Putting aside, for once, identity, and sticking to the writing itself, I remember how, early in my career, a group of writer friends told me I needed to "straighten out" my sentences, that they were too long and convoluted and, as one person put it, "un-American," whatever that means. But it turns out that how I build sentences isn't an affect or style; it's just what I come with, like the face I've got, or how I walk, or how nervous I get around bagpipes and clowns. Of course, if I'm going to be part of a community at all, I don't want unthinking acceptance; I want to be challenged routinely but *meaningfully*, challenged *not* to fit in and be like everyone else, but to be my best *self* as a writer, that is, to be the writer I am and to be respected for that without being allowed to become complacent about it. Aren't the stakes that high? If the community you're part of makes you doubt yourself, wants to change those parts of you that make you you—and make your writing, by extension, uniquely yours—then it's not the right community for you. Keep looking. If you want to. Don't discount, either, the community of one that solitude can be. Alone, as the saying goes, doesn't have to mean lonely. Not that I discount loneliness— indeed, I've found it not the worst thing, now and then, to sit awhile inside it. But for me, alone mostly has meant private; intimate; the place where poems find their start.

The community we need is often not where we expected it.

I've brought up love more than a few times here because,

like finding love, finding the community we need and want requires patience and a bit of luck. And again like love, our relationship to a given community often has a shelf-life; it's not so much that we fail each other, sometimes, but that we can find ourselves traveling in different directions and at different speeds, though for a while we may have been inseparable in our traveling together. Community is an organic thing— unpredictable, therefore, and not necessarily for everyone, not even defined the same way by everyone. Our needs and desires are various as we are, and our writing can't help but distinguish us from others, just as our tastes do, and how we think, versus understand, versus realize a way through—the evidence for which is everything we'll have left behind, be it in the form of art, gesture, whatever differences we made, for better and worse, in the lives of others, some of whom we knew, most of whom we'll never know.

Being a writer has meant living much of my emotional and psychological life in uncertainty, a practice of living in readiness for what I don't yet know, the surprise without which, to my mind, what's the point of writing? To live always in uncertainty, though, would be maddening; an instinct for stability is a survival instinct, even if too much stability can lead to stasis, a lack of resonance: the death of art. As with so many things, then, the key comes down to a careful balancing, in this case between uncertainty and stability. Stability has many forms; different ones work for each of us. For me, as I've mentioned, daily routines (rituals, almost) not ostensibly connected to writing have been essential. But community is also a form of stability, or can be, if we find the right one, at the right time. Some people are part of a writing group, where they share each other's work-in-progress on a regular basis. Alternatively, for many years now I've had exactly one writer friend to whom I show an occasional draft, depending. In the measureless space between those two scenarios, the possibilities are infinite, and include not requiring or longing for community at all, when it comes to writing. It includes, as well, making community of the writing itself. We tend to think of a writing community as a community of writers, but I find I still prefer the community that was the only stable one for me as a kid moving from one town to the next: not writers, but what they've written, and what I myself write in unconscious conversation—again, though, not with the writers but with what they made, guideposts along/talismans for/sometime distractions from the quest that all writers share but must accomplish differently, the quest of making meaning with language, not because we were told to, but because there's no choice in the matter. It's just who we are, and just as mysterious.

ACKNOWLEDGMENTS

I thank the editors of the following journals, where some of these pieces, sometimes in a different form, originally appeared:

Poetry: "Politics" (as "A Politics of Mere Being")

The Sewanee Review: "Ambition," "Stamina"

———

Quotations in the book are from the following sources:

Epigraph: "To envy a wilderness . . . ," Carl Phillips, "The Same in Sun as It Felt in Shadow," *Pale Colors in a Tall Field* (New York: Farrar, Straus & Giroux, 2020)

ACKNOWLEDGMENTS

page 12: "to catch the world / at pure idea," Jorie Graham, "The Nature of Evidence," *Hybrids of Plants and of Ghosts* (Princeton: Princeton University Press, 1980)

page 30: "The deaf don't believe in silence," Ilya Kaminsky, *Deaf Republic* (Minneapolis: Graywolf Press, 2019)

page 42: "The Famous Black Poet . . . ," Carl Phillips, "Passing," *In the Blood* (Boston: Northeastern University Press, 1992)

page 43: "my own stoop- / shouldered kind of blues . . . ," Carl Phillips, "Blue," *In the Blood* (Boston: Northeastern University Press, 1992)

page 54: "Cathedral," Carl Phillips, *Double Shadow* (New York: Farrar, Straus & Giroux, 2011)

page 56: "Finally we forget what we are carrying . . . ," Pamela Alexander, "The Vanishing Point," *Navigable Waterways* (New Haven: Yale University Press, 1985)

page 68: "In this blue light / I can take you there," Jorie Graham, "San Sepolcro," *Erosion* (Princeton: Princeton University Press, 1983)

96

page 68: "You must change your life," Rainer Maria Rilke, *The Book of Fresh Beginnings,* translated by David Young (Oberlin, Ohio: Oberlin College Press, 1994)

page 71: "A way of / crossing a dark . . . ," Carl Phillips, "If a Wilderness," *The Rest of Love* (New York: Farrar, Straus & Giroux, 2004)

page 78: "When she tells her own story . . . ," Carl Phillips, "A Mathematics of Breathing," *Cortège* (Minneapolis: Graywolf Press, 1995)

page 80: "Let us / make of what's left . . . ," Carl Phillips, "In a Perfect World," *Speak Low* (New York: Farrar, Straus & Giroux, 2009)

INDEX